© 2015 YouthLight, Inc. | Chapin, SC 29036
All rights reserved.

Reproduction of any material is strictly prohibited.

Layout by Melody Taylor
Project Editing by Susan Bowman

ISBN: 978-1-59850-168-1
Library of Congress Number: 2014951011
10 9 8 7 6 5 4 3 2 1
Printed in the United States

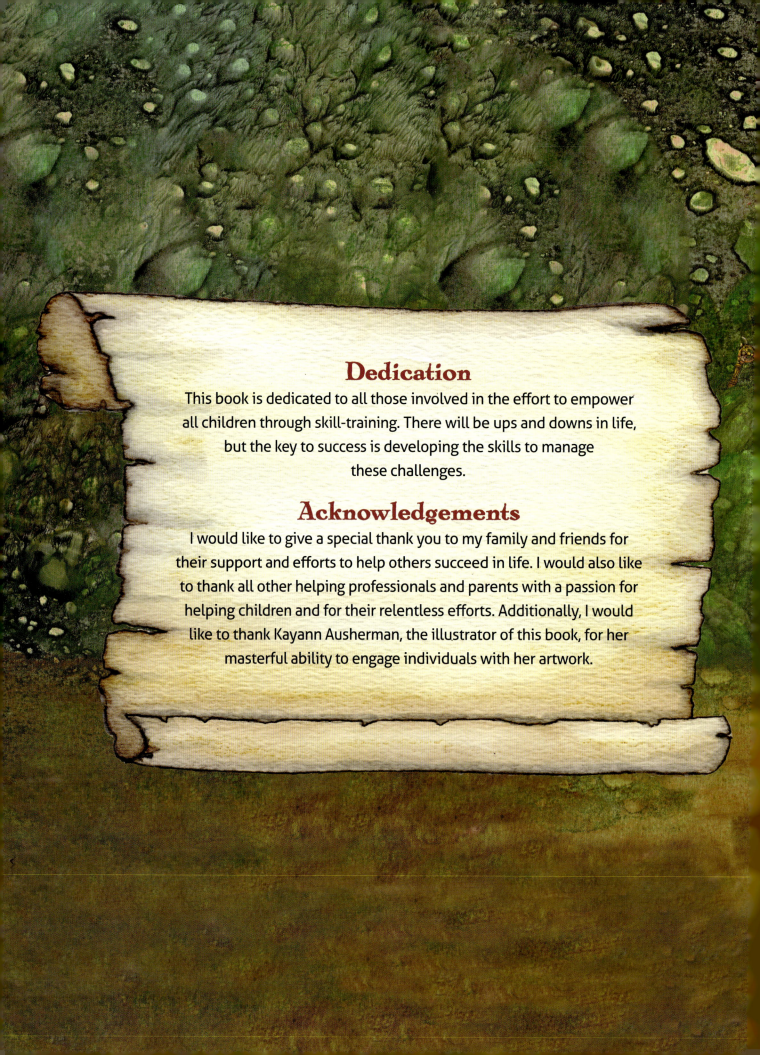

Dedication

This book is dedicated to all those involved in the effort to empower all children through skill-training. There will be ups and downs in life, but the key to success is developing the skills to manage these challenges.

Acknowledgements

I would like to give a special thank you to my family and friends for their support and efforts to help others succeed in life. I would also like to thank all other helping professionals and parents with a passion for helping children and for their relentless efforts. Additionally, I would like to thank Kayann Ausherman, the illustrator of this book, for her masterful ability to engage individuals with her artwork.

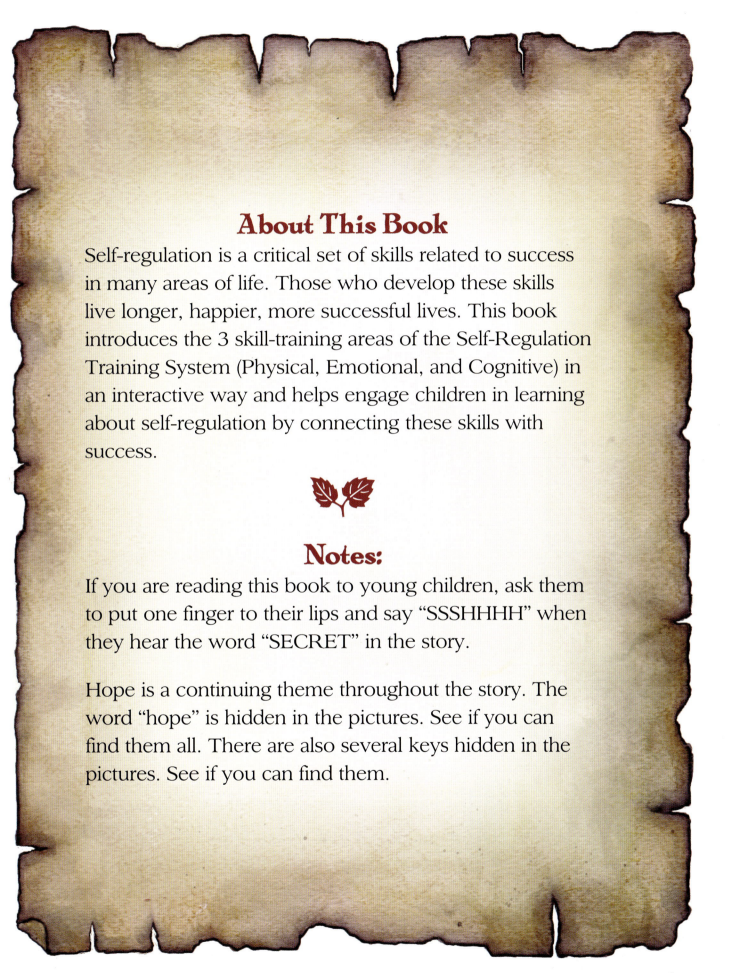

About This Book

Self-regulation is a critical set of skills related to success in many areas of life. Those who develop these skills live longer, happier, more successful lives. This book introduces the 3 skill-training areas of the Self-Regulation Training System (Physical, Emotional, and Cognitive) in an interactive way and helps engage children in learning about self-regulation by connecting these skills with success.

Notes:

If you are reading this book to young children, ask them to put one finger to their lips and say "SSSHHHH" when they hear the word "SECRET" in the story.

Hope is a continuing theme throughout the story. The word "hope" is hidden in the pictures. See if you can find them all. There are also several keys hidden in the pictures. See if you can find them.

In a village far, far away, there once lived three men who were very old, very wise and very happy. They knew each other because they had done so many great things together and had lived so long. They met down by the lake every week to talk about how they had all lived such long and happy lives. They called themselves THE REGULATORS. These three men created a SECRET list of skills that helped them to be happy, successful and healthy. The Regulators spent their days teaching these SECRETS to all the children in their village. The village was called Balance and it was a very happy place to live.

In a nearby village lived a very different group of people. They were a very sad and angry bunch. They were called the OOC. OOC stands for Out of Control. One night a group of OOCs attacked the village of Balance. They captured two of the Regulators, but the third escaped with the list of SECRETS. He snuck away and disappeared with the list of SECRETS. The legend says that he carefully hid parts of the list in three secret places for someone, someday to find and teach to children once again. Neither the Regulators nor the list of SECRETS were seen or heard from again….

Many, many years later a very kind man named Tomas, who lived in a small village with his wife, had a baby boy and a baby girl. They were twins. Tomas and his wife wished every night for their children to live long, healthy, happy lives. They had heard about the legend of the Regulators and their SECRET list.

One night, Tomas was in the attic looking for some of his baby clothes to give to his son, when he found an old, rusty, metal box that his great-great-grandfather had left him. He hadn't looked inside the box for many years and decided to open it.

Inside, he found an old piece of paper with a picture of three old men sitting by a lake. "Who were these men?" he wondered. Tomas held the picture up to the light to take a closer look.

On the back of the picture he discovered that there was some writing. It said:

There is a SECRET list.
Follow these clues to find what others have missed.
If you find this list and do these things,
You'll have all the happiness this life brings.

{CLUE #1}
In this place of dark and mist,
You'll find the first page of the list.
When your body's ALARM
 starts to sound,
As your heart begins to
 pound,
Remember to breathe.
 This isn't a race.
Calm is the key to finding
your SAFE PLACE.

Tomas shouted, "I can't believe it! I've found it! It's a clue to the Regulator's Secret List!" He had wished every day for his children to live long, healthy, happy lives. Now, he had found a way to make it happen.

Deep down in his heart Tomas knew he needed to follow the clue and try his best to find the SECRET list of the Regulators. He had heard his grandfather talk about a place by the sea called the Caves of Calm. He decided that this would be a good place to start looking. Tomas packed a bag and kissed his family good-bye as he set out on his quest to find the pages to the SECRET list.

After three days of searching, Tomas found the entrance to the Caves of Calm. As he entered, he noticed the heavy mist inside the cave. It was so thick that he couldn't see very far at all. He came to a large opening. Tomas knew he must be getting close.

Now in front of him was a very narrow bridge leading over a deep, dark crack in the earth. As he tested the bridge, he quickly discovered that if he made one wrong step, he would fall down into the deep, deep hole. He pulled out the picture he had found in the attic with the clues written on the back. He read the first clue out loud:

In this place of dark and mist,
You'll find the first SECRET of the list.
When your body's ALARM starts to sound,
As your heart begins to pound,
Remember to breathe.
This isn't a race.
Calm is the key to finding your SAFE PLACE.

He could feel his body's ALARM starting to sound. He was scared. His heart was racing. His stomach felt sick. His head began to ache. His thoughts were cloudy. At that moment, he understood what the clue meant. Tomas needed to be calm and focused to cross the bridge through the mist.

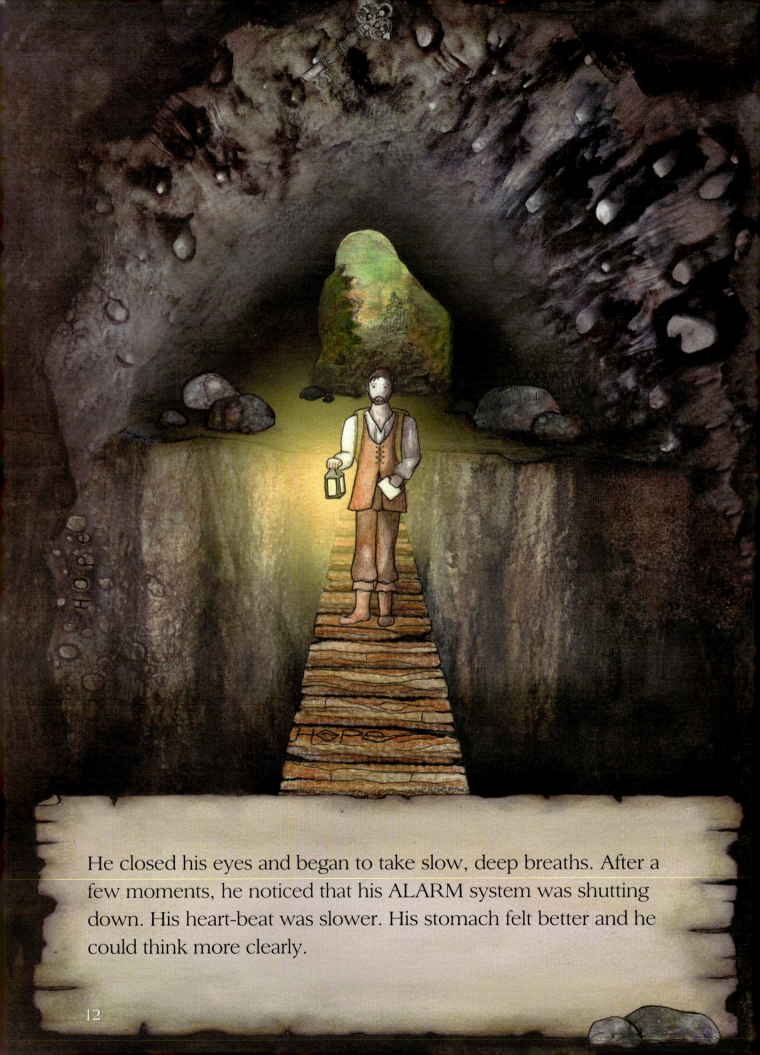

He closed his eyes and began to take slow, deep breaths. After a few moments, he noticed that his ALARM system was shutting down. His heart-beat was slower. His stomach felt better and he could think more clearly.

He calmly crossed the bridge, and on the other side he found an old, dusty chest with a torn piece of paper inside. It said:

The Regulators' SECRET List

{SECRET #1}
Learn your Warning Signs and learn how to Calm them down to feel Safe.

On the back, the paper also had a clue for finding the next SECRET. It read:

{CLUE #2}

In this place of trees and sadness,
You'll find the second SECRET if you can survive the madness.
Feelings are a powerful thing.
They are why we cry and why we sing.
Feelings can be hard to see,
Giving them a name helps solve the mystery.
We can bottle them up or let them come bursting out,
Finding balance is what the SECRET list is about.
You must take control of what is yours.
Don't be a boat in the water without any oars.

As Tomas read the words, he began to think of place he had heard of as a child. It was a place he was warned never to go…
The Dark Forest of Feelings.

The Dark Forest of Feelings was a dangerous place. Tomas had heard that many who entered this forest never returned. It was said that the Forest could make people feel so hopeless and lonely that they gave up their will to live. But Tomas wanted his two children to live long, healthy, happy lives so much that he decided to go on with his quest. He set out for The Dark Forest of Feelings the very next morning.

After traveling for two days, Tomas reached the edge of the forest. He sat down, opened his backpack and took out some food and a picture of his family. He remembered why he was on this quest and how important it was for him to find the SECRET list. When he finished his snack, he picked up his pack and bravely entered the forest.

Even though it was a bright sunny day, the forest seemed very dark. Tomas could hear strange sounds all around him. They sounded like whispers, but he didn't see any people. Tomas walked for several hours in the forest. He noticed that he was feeling very weak and very tired. His muscles were hurting more than they ever had before. He was also starting to understand what the whispers were saying. They were saying things like:

"You're not going to make it. It's too hard." "You're a loser." "Quit trying." "It's hopeless."

"You will be lost forever." "You'll never find it and your children will fail."

Tomas was starting to feel overwhelmed by his pain and a strong hopeless feeling. He finally fell to his knees. He could go no further. Tomas opened his pack to get something to eat, and he saw the paper with Clue #2 written on it.

He took it out and read the clue again:

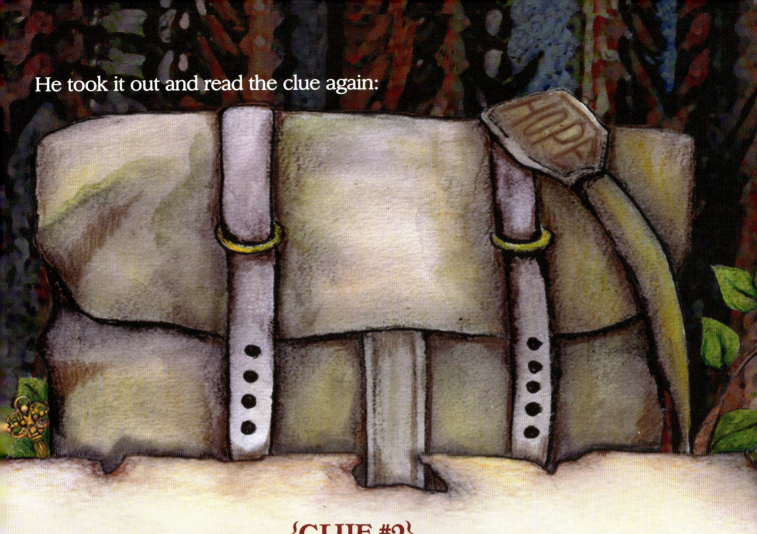

{CLUE #2}

In this place of trees and sadness,
You'll find the second SECRET if you can survive
the madness.
Feelings are a powerful thing.
They are why we cry and why we sing.
Feelings can be hard to see,
Giving them a name helps solve the mystery.
We can bottle them up or let them come bursting out,
Finding balance is what the SECRET list is about.
You must take control of what is yours.
Don't be a boat in the water without any oars.

After he read it, Tomas thought about the words for a moment. He realized that he was letting the dark forest get to him. He decided he needed to take action. He needed to give the feelings he was having a name. He said aloud, "I feel SAD." Right after he said it, he began to feel better because he knew he had felt sad before and that it doesn't last forever. Then he thought, just as the clue said, he must let the feeling out. He took out of his pack a pen and a piece of paper and began to write down how he felt. Tomas quickly started to feel more energy come back to him and his mood got better.

Next, he decided that he was in control of his feelings and the whispers in the forest could not change his mood if he didn't allow it. Just then, he noticed a lighted path leading through the forest. It began to shine brightly. It must have been there all the time, but he just couldn't see it because of his sadness. With his new energy, he jumped to his feet, grabbed his pack and began to sing as he followed the trail of lights.

The trail led him to the other edge of the forest, where he found a small, wooden box sitting on a stone table. He opened the box to find a torn piece of paper. It was SECRET #2. It read:

{SECRET #2}
Learn to label and express your feelings in healthy ways. Understand that your feelings are yours and that nothing can MAKE you feel scared, sad, or angry unless you allow it.

On the back, the paper also had the Clue for finding the final SECRET. It read:

{CLUE #3}

In this place of twists and turns,
You will find the third SECRET for which your heart yearns.
Watch your thinking along the way,
Or lost in the maze forever you will stay.
You are what you think. Remember that.
Healthy thoughts will get you to where the last SECRET is at.
When we have a plan we're at our best,
Change your thoughts to solve the problem and finish the quest.

Tomas thought about the clue for a moment. He remembered reading a story once about a place called the Labyrinth of Lies.

The Labyrinth of Lies was a place where bushes grew in thick rows that created a giant maze. People that went into the maze would not come back for many days. And if they did return, they were often much different than when they went in. He remembered the story telling of a very nice man who went into the maze. When he finally made it out, he was so angry that he yelled and threw things at his own family and friends. He died shortly after… angry and alone.

Note: A labyrinth is a very large maze made of bushes. It's so big you could get lost inside.

Tomas thought again about his twins back home and decided to enter the Labyrinth of Lies to face the dangers of the maze. After walking for only a few minutes, he saw a golden jar sitting on top of a tree stump in the distance. He couldn't believe his eyes. He was so excited that he began to run toward it. But the faster he ran, the farther away the jar seemed to get. Tomas was starting to get frustrated. He ran until he couldn't take another step. It was getting dark. He was exhausted and fell asleep.

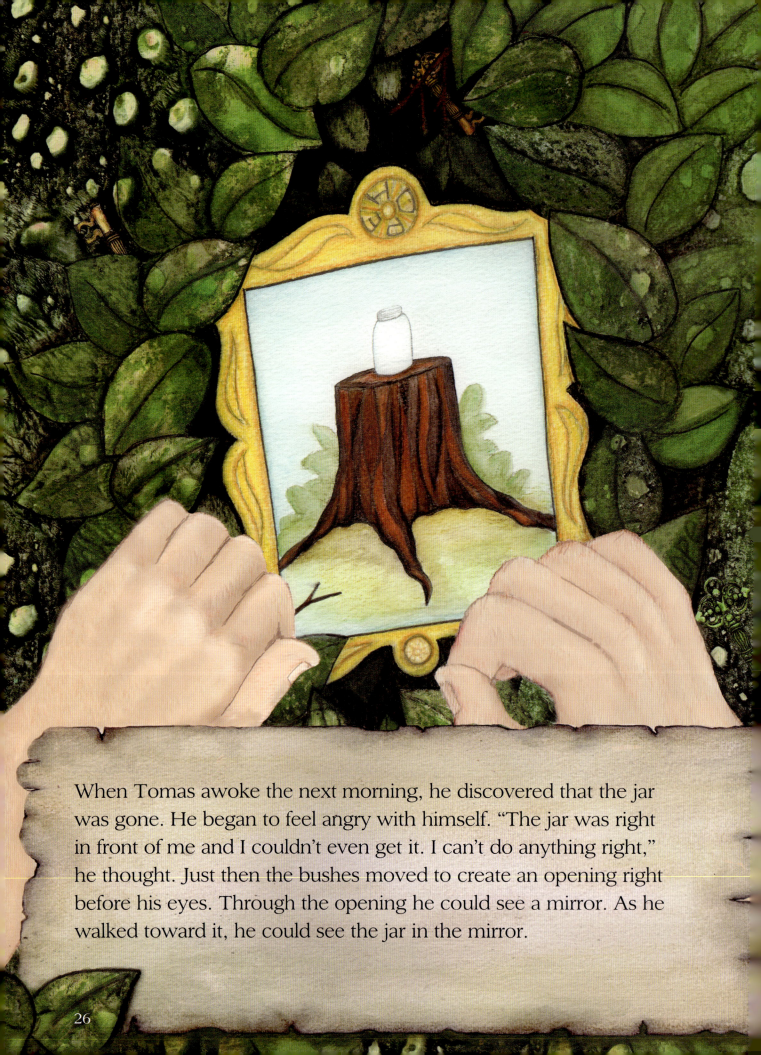

When Tomas awoke the next morning, he discovered that the jar was gone. He began to feel angry with himself. "The jar was right in front of me and I couldn't even get it. I can't do anything right," he thought. Just then the bushes moved to create an opening right before his eyes. Through the opening he could see a mirror. As he walked toward it, he could see the jar in the mirror.

As he stepped through the opening, he noticed that there were mirrors all over in the bushes for as far as he could see in both directions. He could see the jar's reflection in all of the mirrors, so he knew that if he followed them, he would reach the real jar. He decided to walk to his left, breaking the mirrors as he went along.

After hours of walking and breaking mirrors, Tomas began to get very frustrated again. He thought, "This maze is against me. The whole world is against me. I hate this place and everything in it." He began to kick and smash the mirrors in anger until he finally fell to the ground and went to sleep.

The next morning, Tomas woke up in a very angry mood with pieces of broken mirrors all around him. He was still thinking very angry thoughts about the maze and about everything that had happened. He decided to give up on the mirrors and walk back the way he had come. When he turned around he saw a very short, old woman. Right away, he began to think angry thoughts about her like, "She's never going to help me. Nobody ever helps me. I hate her."

The old woman noticed Tomas and slowly walked over to him. She said, "Hello. My name is Hope. Can I help you?" Tomas replied in a very angry, loud, rude voice, "How could you ever help me? Nobody ever helps me! I hate this place and everything in it!" Hope sadly turned and walked away.

Tomas looked down at the ground and saw his reflection in a piece of a broken mirror. He was surprised to see how angry his face looked. He almost didn't recognize himself. It was at that moment he realized how angry he had become and how angry his thoughts were. He pulled Clue #3 from his pocket and read it aloud.

{CLUE #3}

In this place of twists and turns,
You will find the third SECRET for which your heart yearns.
Watch your thinking along the way,
Or lost in the maze forever you will stay.
You are what you think. Remember that.
Healthy thoughts will get you to where the last SECRET is at.
When we have a plan we're at our best,
Change your thoughts to solve the problem and finish the quest.

After reading the clue again, Tomas realized that his thoughts were causing his angry feelings and that's why he treated the old woman so very badly. He looked up and saw her about to disappear into the maze and he ran as fast as he could to catch her. When Tomas reached Hope, he said, "I'm so sorry. I understand that my thoughts have gotten very angry and I'm sorry I let myself treat you that way. Can you please help me? I'm looking for a special jar and for the way out of this maze."

Hope said, "I understand and I'm so glad you figured out that you can control your thoughts and change them. I saw a small jar just down the way," as she turned and pointed down a lighted path. In a helpful voice she said, "Take the first right turn after you reach the jar and you will find the exit to the maze."

Tomas thanked her and followed her directions. He found the jar and ran to the exit. After Tomas was safely out of the maze, he opened the jar and found a piece of torn paper with writing on it. It read:

{SECRET #3}

Learn to keep watch over your thoughts, for they are powerful and can lead you to feel sad, angry, or scared. You control your thoughts and can change them to be more helpful if you choose to.

Tomas had completed his quest. He was so excited to have all three pieces of the Regulators' SECRET list. He began the long journey home. It had been almost a month since Tomas started his journey. When he finally reached his village, he ran to his home to see his family. His wife and children were so happy to see him!

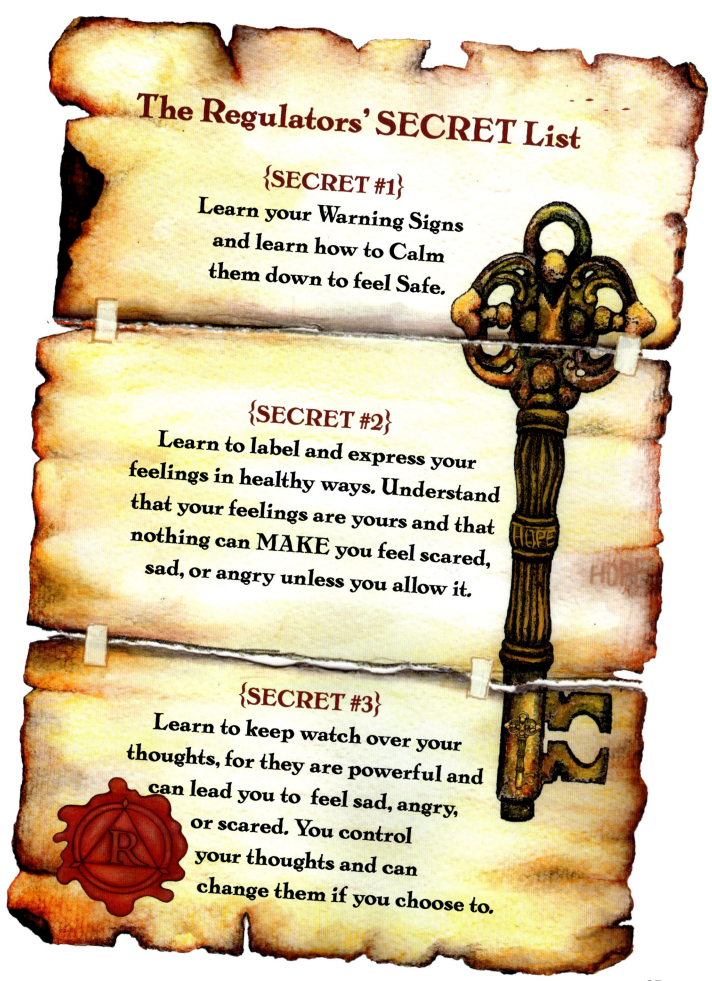

The Regulators' SECRET List

{SECRET #1}
Learn your Warning Signs and learn how to Calm them down to feel Safe.

{SECRET #2}
Learn to label and express your feelings in healthy ways. Understand that your feelings are yours and that nothing can MAKE you feel scared, sad, or angry unless you allow it.

{SECRET #3}
Learn to keep watch over your thoughts, for they are powerful and can lead you to feel sad, angry, or scared. You control your thoughts and can change them if you choose to.

Over the next several years, Tomas worked very hard to teach his children, and the other children in the village, the skills he had learned from the Regulators' SECRET List.

> The Legend of the Regulators is an engaging way to introduce Self-Regulation skills to children. We want to share these SECRETS to a long, healthy, happy life.

Healthy Self-Regulation skills are highly related to success and happiness. These skills can be taught and practiced in a systematic way to help individuals gain the tools necessary for success in many areas of life. The Self-Regulation Training System breaks these skills down into three skill-training areas:

{SECRET #1}
Learn your Warning Signs and learn how to Calm them down to feel Safe.

{SECRET #2}
Learn to label and express your feelings in healthy ways. Understand that your feelings are yours and that nothing can MAKE you feel scared, sad, or angry unless you allow it.

{SECRET #3}
Learn to keep watch over your thoughts, for they are powerful and can lead you to feel sad, angry, or scared. You control your thoughts and can change them if you choose to.

PHYSICAL
- Learn your body's early warning signs of upset
- Master the calming skills and create a sense of safety to shut down the body's warning system

EMOTIONAL
- Learn to label your feelings
- Learn to express your feelings in healthy ways
- Learn that you own your feelings and that other people/things cannot make you feel a certain way

COGNITIVE
- Learn to identify and challenge extreme, unhealthy thoughts
- Learn to get your needs met in healthy ways
- Learn to use basic planning, problem-solving, and organizational skills

TIP: Design your behavioral reinforcement system to target these skills after they have been taught and practiced.

DISCUSSION QUESTIONS:

1. What were some of Tomas' warning signs in the Caves of Calm? How did he calm himself?

2. If one of your friends or family members were having warning signs, what could you do to help them?

3. What was Tomas feeling in the Dark Forest of Feelings? How was he able to help himself?

4. How did Tomas change his thoughts to get the jar in the Labyrinth of Lies?

5. How will SECRET #1 help you have a happy life? In school? With friends? With your family?

6. How will SECRET #2 help you have a happy life? In school? With friends? With your family?

7. How will SECRET #3 help you have a happy life? In school? With friends? With your family?

8. How is Hope a theme throughout the story?

Suggested Activities for Physical Regulation Skills {SECRET #1}

Remember when Tomas was about to cross the bridge in the Caves of Calm? He was scared and his body's ALARM was telling him that he was starting to get upset. We all have an alarm system in our body that tells us when we are starting to become sad, angry or scared. Our body gives us Warning Signs when we are starting to get upset. What were some of the Warning Signs Tomas had in the Caves of Calm?

- Try to list as many of your own "warning signs" as you can?
- Over the next few days, try to look for "warning signs" that you may see in other people.

When Tomas discovered that his body's ALARM was sounding and his Warning Signs were starting, he knew that this would not help him cross the bridge. How was he able to turn off his body's ALARM? Once we learn to listen to our body's Warning Signs, the first SECRET also tells us that we need to learn and practice ways to turn off our ALARM.

- Create a list of your favorite ways to help yourself feel calm, safe and relaxed?
- Ask your friends and family what they do to calm themselves down when they feel upset.
- Describe three places you like to go to feel calm and safe.

{SECRET #1}
Learn your Warning Signs and learn how to Calm them down to feel Safe.

Suggested Activities for Emotional Regulation Skills {SECRET #2}

Remember when Tomas was in the Forest of Feelings and he started to get upset? He didn't know what was wrong and things seemed hopeless. Then he realized that he was feeling sad and he was letting this feeling get him down. This was not helping him finish his quest. The CLUE reminded him that he needed to say how he was feeling and let his feelings out in a healthy way. Just as SECRET #2 says, Tomas realized that he had the power to name, express and take control of his feelings.

- Name as many feelings as you can.

- List healthy ways to express each feeling you named.

- Have a simple discussion about whether or not other people and things can "make" us feel a certain way. Use examples and promote the idea that other people and things can have some influence, but we decide what to feel, how intense the feeling is and how long we feel that way.

{SECRET #2}
Learn to label and express your feelings in healthy ways. Understand that your feelings are yours and that nothing can MAKE you feel scared, sad, or angry unless you allow it.

Suggested Activities for Cognitive Regulation Skills {SECRET #3}

Remember when Tomas was in the Labyrinth of Lies and he started to become upset and break the mirrors? He was having some very strong thoughts that were not helping him reach his goal. His thoughts also caused him to treat Hope very badly. Then, just like the 3rd SECRET says, Tomas learned that he can control his thoughts and change them if they aren't helping.

- Discuss some examples of thoughts that can get in our way and how we might be able to change those thoughts to be more helpful (ex. – Nobody likes me. Nothing I do is good enough.).

- Generate ideas about healthy vs. unhealthy ways to get our emotional/psychological needs met (ex. – the need for attention).

- Review basic Problem-solving steps.

- Talk about how organization and making plans can help us reach our goals.

{SECRET #3}
Learn to label and express your feelings in healthy ways. Understand that your feelings are yours and that nothing can MAKE you feel scared, sad, or angry unless you allow it.

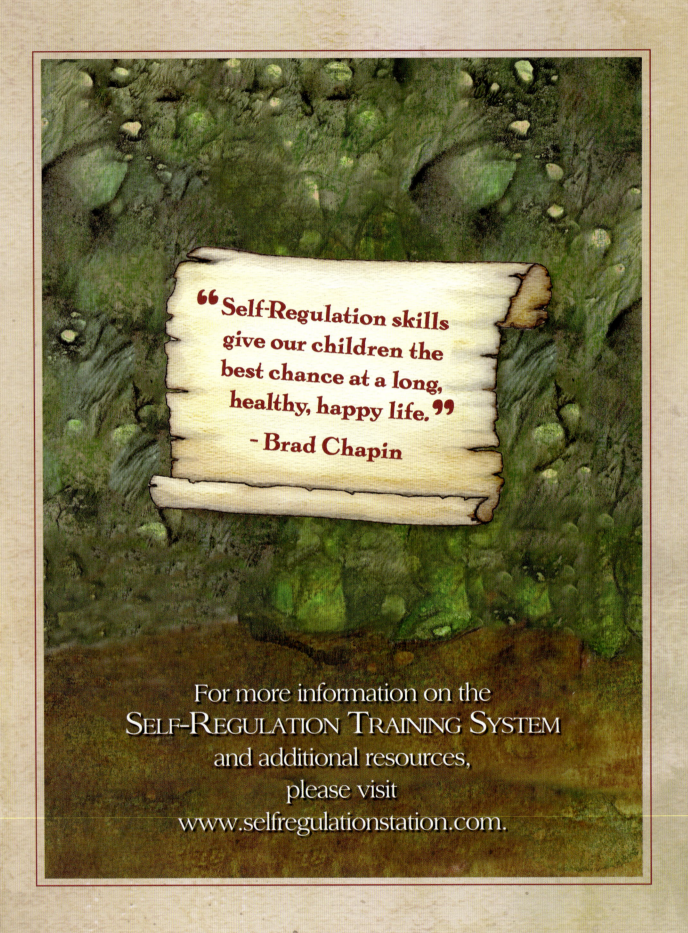